The Colors of My Life

The Brighter Colors are Gifts from God

By

Benaiah Harris

Copyright 2022 -The Colors of My Life

The Brighter Colors are Gifts from God

by Benaiah Harris

Dedication

FIRST TO JESUS CHRIST THE HEAD OF MY LIFE

My Mother - Sybil Harris

**Brothers and Sisters - Marcia Harris, Jeffrey Harris &
Richard Harris**

&

Myself - Diane (Benaiah) Harris

*We were all there keeping each other in love in the days
of our father's abuse.*

2

Table of Contents

Introduction

The days of Benaiah Harris are days that anyone of us can relate to, but only to a certain extent. We have relationships, children, and God, all of which you will read about.

What you will want to read about is how she survived the death of two sons, the abuse of her father (dad), and at the time she was burnt by her own efforts to stop her dad's abuse.

The coming into Christ is going to be the highlight as you read on and the way she found God is nothing but a miracle. One that was reserved just for her in her own story. You are also awaiting a miracle. As you get into alignment with Benaiah's testimony, the revelations for yourself will become even clearer than ever.

This does mean what you think it means. It means you will be touched in the deepest part of your heart as God works the story of others for the good and from a place of love.

There are many books of how people find Christ and become anew but Benaiah has not just found Christ, she has fully aligned her life inside and out. Take her words as not just a testimony but as true guidance of how this can be you. Not just any you but the God in you.

Recalling when I was in a relationship, trying to do what I wanted in my life meaning certain rules did not apply to me. I led a life that morally was not of God and even with all the sin, I still loved God without really knowing who he was. The truth is, I was in love with the Lord but the ways of the world, pulled heavily on me.

Even with my love for our Lord and Savior, I would crave him deeply to the point I became a bible thief. This sounds funny but was so true and I was not even aware of what I was doing. Every time I would travel and stay in hotels, the first thing I would look for in the room is a bible. When I tell this story, many people laugh but if there was a bible, it was going home with me. I ended up having so many bibles that until this day, I have boxes of them.

At that time, I was still in sin but my craving for God was pulling on my heart hard and I was fighting against it. But that would all soon change for Pastor Benaiah Harris.

On a faithful day in 2007, a friend of mine had a ticket for me and my brother to fly out to Florida and celebrate Memorial Day. I was getting excited and looking forward to partying in Florida but that pulling on my heart was deeper than ever. I ended up going to the altar in Philadelphia, giving my life over to God and all who knew me, was in amazement to know this had happened. They were out partying in Florida and trying to see where I was while I was getting baptized.

This is a testimony of what God can do and when he is in control of our lives. When he states, enough is enough, we must give in. This was 14 years ago, and my life has been life changing in so many ways. I have been tested even more with my faith in so many ways, but God always showed up. It has been the best thing I have ever done and could not see my life without our Father. I have been running with God and will never look back at who Diane Harris was before getting saved.

In 2011, my Lord and savior decided it was time for another change which was my name. He named me Benaiah which biblically is a boy's name of Hebrew Origin which means "Built by God". By granting me this name, this was God's gift to symbolize the loyalty I have for him due to conquering of all the trials and tribulations I had to withstand.

With God promises and faithfulness, he gifted me again on August 15, 2018, with my phone ministry, Seeds of Blessings Prayer Line. This prayer line represents all believers and like-minded individuals, wanting to glorify our father in every area of our lives.

All the "I" in my story are one to many however they are an important part of my testimony as the "I" became a trilogy of God: The Father, Daughter: Me and Jesus: Holy Spirit/Christ. The story is one of sacrifice, stubbornness and faith all working together to reinvent me to who I AM.

Colors as A Key

The colors that I assigned each Chapter represent how God has used colors in my life. Every event or memorable experience can be seen by the colors of life. When you see a color that you can relate to then you are in for a surprise. The colors of darkness are the ones that you will start to see the light. Not only are the colors of my life a good representation of how things were going during those times, but they are also a good representation of the lighter days to come.

Choices are important to paint your day the right color. Learning new colors is also important as looking at an old paint job can get very depressing so change up your colors to where you are excited to see the day, not trying to cover it up.

I call it color coding with God. You can brighten up your life and be happy in Christ or you can use your power of water paint where the color fades with any brush of water. Oil is thicker than water and anointed oil is everlasting.

Brown - Tears & Sadness
Blue - Loyalty & Trust
Black – Hardship, Pain & Suffering
Purple - Transformation
Green - Growth & Strength
Rainbow - Revelation

Red - Life Changing
Bright Red - Action
Orange - Transition
Yellow – Wisdom
Gold – Glory, Grace & Divinity

The Dying Days (Pre Christ)

BLACK: Hardship, Pain and Suffering
RAINBOW COLOR: Revelation

I was born in Kingston, Jamaica on the 5th of October 1963 to Hubert and Sybil Harris. I had two sisters and three brothers two of which were half brother and sister. We were a family who used to go to church twice on Sunday and sometimes during the midweek.

Growing up my dad was an alcoholic, he was a good father when he was not drunk, but when he drank it was hell to pay in my house. My mother, on the other hand, was soft-spoken and loved our dad so much that no matter the abuse she would not leave him and if she did leave my dad would come and get us when he was sober and apologize. He would buy us new stuff and our mother would go back home only to repeat the same thing again. My mother was beaten.

Everyone knows my dad and when he is drunk all the neighbors would hear his mouth a million miles away. Sometimes we were beaten, and the neighbors would call the cops and my mother would tell them I can't leave him because of the children. We were very young, and this abuse continued into our adult life.

My older brother took to the streets and became one of the bad boys out there just because he did not know how to

9

help at the time to stop my dad from beating my mom. My mom was a beautiful woman who bore many scars on her outside as well as her inside.

Alcoholism was the driving force for my dad. It made him cruel, and I was afraid of him. I lived a life of agony and was so afraid of my dad that at the sound of his voice I would pee on myself. No child should live through the pain my siblings and I have lived through.

As I begin to grow older I started to look for love but we were not allowed to go anywhere not even Church, by this time as the years pass my parents were no longer going to Church so that means we were not going either so when our friends would come and ask for us to come too my dad would either say, "They have not washed the dishes yet." or whatever he chose to say at that time. My mother wouldn't dare say anything or she would be beaten depending on his mood. I really loved my dad despite his drinking habits and the abuse. He was a good provider and my mother did not have to work. Her job was to stay home and take care of her family; my mother never had friends except one or two and she never went to any of their homes, she would go to the market and back home. My dad was a contractor who builds some of the most beautiful homes and would design blueprints for every home he ever built.

My dad also had affairs and had a son outside of his marriage. Years after he brought his child home for my mother to raise him, at that time I was about sixteen and had my first child Marlon who was killed at age twenty-six, his dad was the love of my life Martin F. his parents were very wealthy, and my dad liked him because he was from a good family with a good background. He went into the army before I got pregnant and I was at my dance class one night when I looked up and saw Carlton, that shiny bicycle he used to ride, and I ran out of the class to greet him. He had just gotten home from the army.

When our son Marlon, who is deceased, was three years old the love of my life and my son's dad was killed in the army. My life was never the same. He was a young man with great ambition and was killed at the age of twenty-four, almost the same age as our son when he was killed.

Now by this time I was still in my parent's house watching my mom and dad still fussing and fighting until one day my sister, brother, and I decided that we can't sit and watch our mom being beaten anymore so we took matters into our own hands and that day we were all burned up. My little brother and my dad were wrestling and my sister and I went to help him and my sister had a pot of hot water coming in and I didn't see her behind the door. The door was pushed and we were all badly burned except my little brother. My dad and sister got burned the most.

After witnessing all I did, I became a runner and didn't even know it. It just happened. I had made up my mind that no man would ever treat me like my dad treated my mom, so at the slightest disagreement with anyone, I was gone and I didn't care how much they loved me. If you look like someone who was abusive, I was gone. I was not sticking around to work anything out. All that time I did not know that I was wounded from the inside. All I know is that no man will ever put his hands on me.

Later I fell in love again and got pregnant with a guy and had my daughter Sarnia who is now forty, her dad also was killed riding a motorcycle when she was about two years old so now, I have two children with deceased fathers.

You would think that's it but still searching for love while still living in my parent's house. I was a very pretty girl with a messed-up life now meeting another guy we called him P, which was his last name. Thinking that I was in love again, I got pregnant twice more, neither of them did I keep. I had two abortions, but P was an alcoholic just like my dad only he was not abusive like my dad.

By this time my dad and mom were separated and my siblings and I were home with mom still living there. My sister had a boyfriend that had a sister and I became friends with her and one day I went to her house and while I was there one Sunday afternoon a car pulled up with my sister's ex and there was this guy in the car staring at me and I was staring at him too. He inquired who I was and we started to see each other. Still searching for love, the relationship got serious and we were together for eight years and that was baby daddy number three. By the time my son was about four we separated, the guy wanted to fight because I wanted to leave him. He did not want to work and I was tired of working and taking care of my son with help from his parents. It was their first grandchild and he was spoiled and still is up to this day. He was born with a gold spoon in his mouth, that's an old saying and I needed to find my own gold spoon. Still looking for love…

I am back in my parent's house after baby daddy number three. I then met a young man and we loved each other. We were an item for over a year until one night we were coming from his grandmother's and I saw some suspicious activity as this car went by. I told him to let us turn and he insisted to keep going, we ended up getting held up by gunmen and we did not see which way he ran. I was dragged into some bushes as they told me they want to see what their leader wants to do with me. I was crying while they began to strip off all my jewelry and all I could hear was the sound of my boyfriend who ran away crying out at the top of his lungs.

The guys finally got to a big tree where their leader was hiding. Now by this time all I could see in my mind is my body with bullets floating into the water. The next day, even though I did not know then that God was on my side, the leader told them to let me go. In the dark bushes, I began to run while falling multiple times crying while waiting to hear the sound of a gunshot in my back.

God saved me even though I was not serving him. They did not rape me or harm me. All they did was rob me and by the time I found my way back to the top of the road the police were there and started to ask me questions and I asked them to take me home. I never wanted to see my boyfriend again and that was it because I told him what I saw and he did not listen and let me go into the trap and then ran away leaving me. After that, there was no peace for me. He would come to my house every day crying for me to take him back but that was it for me. Still looking for love…

Now after that I met baby daddy number four who was dark and handsome and did not have two nickels to make a dime, but I was not looking for money at that time. I was searching for love in all the wrong places, that relationship lasted for less than a year and baby number four was on the way, my precious Son who died a year ago.

Still in my parent's home, back in Jamaica, we weren't in a hurry to leave our parent's house. My other kids were with their grandparents and I felt like I didn't have any kids and didn't look like I had any either. It seems as if the more kids I had the better I looked, sin really looked good when you don't know any better.

So now I met an older man who used to treat me really well and was the first one to send me overseas. We dated for a while and went overseas to do business. He helped me to get a business license and tried to teach me how to save money as I did not have this skill at this point in my life but now, I had my own place. He was trying to help me purchase a house and teach me how to come up with some of the money, but I did not care to learn at that time. Instead of investing the money, I was shopping for my kids and family, and he did not help me to purchase the house, so we ended up parting ways. Every now and then we would get together until we were no more.

Still looking for love in the wrong places, I met a man, baby daddy number five. It was an adulterous affair that lasted for ten years and almost cost me my life, in this relationship I got everything I wanted. A house in one of the best neighborhoods money could pay for, a reserved parking spot with twenty-four-hour security. I didn't even have to open my gate. I had my private rental car company, while running one of his businesses, traveling anytime I wanted. This man has money and can do and buy anything he wants. He spoiled me. If I needed a new car, all I had to do is say it but all that was at the price of my soul because I was living in sin. Even after accumulating all the material stuff and still having to spend my nights and holidays lonely, loneliness started to wear on me and I couldn't go anywhere without him randomly popping up. Even if he knew where I was going, we would take different cars and he followed me from time to time.

At first, I didn't mind but as the years go by, I didn't like it because I was controlled and constantly been monitored, not that I was doing anything, but he didn't trust me because after
a while I found out that I wasn't his only mistress, but I am the one he couldn't do without. He could trust me with his money and his business, everyone else just wanted his money. This relationship went on as I said for years, one day one of my son's aunts told me what my son said, and it made me feel bad because as a little boy he was thinking of

that kind of stuff. It made him not like the man he knew from a young age. He wanted his mom to have someone for herself and he was afraid of me getting old and being alone. No kid should have to carry that burden so over time I was planning a way to get out of that situation.

While I was planning to leave Jamaica, I found out that I was pregnant with baby number five and still not married. My son had no idea that his aunt told me that information but at that moment I knew I had to do something so when I found out I was pregnant I knew I would leave.

What I did not mention is that I became friends with his wife and I told him I felt like a hypocrite but the truth of the matter is I had such a great love for him, I fell in love with his wife and kids and she loved me too. Even when I tried to stay away, she would always try to call me for advice about her husband I was with too. I knew he was cheating on both of us because she would tell me what he did or what he is not doing. I would argue with him on her behalf and tell him how I feel and sometimes he would be on his phone talking to her in my presence and shouting at her and I would argue with him about talking to her like that in front of me.

Knowing what I was doing was wrong, but sin never looks bad when you are in it, yes you have a conscience but that doesn't stop you until you have an awakening from the Lord. Now it's time for me to make a hard decision since I now know I am pregnant and need to leave. I convinced him that I needed to go away to have my baby but now it

seems like, why do you need his permission to leave?
Well, you can't just walk away from someone so powerful, especially when you are caring for his child, so I had to be diplomatic!! I had learned from him the best LOL.

Now we must agree that I will go away and have my baby and I know once I get here there is nothing he could do. Well, so I thought, until after I had the baby and he realized I am not getting along with him like I used to, he had bought me a car before I had the baby, got me an apartment, and now after having my baby I am going to work with AT&T. One day I went and got another apartment, paid for it, arranged to pick up the moving trucks, and had the guys ready to help me during my lunch break before he came.

He would normally come to America every two weeks because he was a businessman and he could come as often as he wanted, but this particular day in question he showed up earlier than I anticipated. It's almost like he knew something was wrong but when you are with someone for ten years, they know you and when I started to act differently it wasn't sitting well with him. The truth be told I was telling him I need to go but he wasn't trying to hear that. As a matter of fact, he didn't think I would have the guts to walk away from so much but after a while, everything does not matter when all you want is freedom.

I was tired of the life I was living and wanted to stop but he wasn't trying to hear any of it. I had to do it for me and especially my kids and my son who this was affecting even though he didn't think I knew. That day I planned to move before he showed up however, he showed up before I had a chance to move. Prior to that he came and was trying to argue with me but while we were arguing my son, who was my firstborn, called and heard me crying. He was upset with him on the phone and after my son hung up, he wanted to fight with me. It quickly reminded how I saw my dad physically abuse my mom I said, "No man will ever put their hands on me."

I ran out of the apt at that time I was in Florida, I ran out and left my son who was a newborn in the apartment. I left my cell phone and went to stay with a friend, we work together. She was really my brother's friend, but we became friends too, so he called everyone on my cell phone even this guy that had liked me and he didn't want the drama or to be killed so he walked away. Anyway, I planned my move again and he showed up again so this time I spoke to the guys who were going to help me and let them know to wait until tomorrow so that night I did not go home to that apartment I went to the new apartment which I already paid for and had the keys so that evening after work I picked up my baby from the sitter and went to Walmart bought stuff for the apartment and change of clothes for me and my baby. He called me twenty-one times that night and I did not answer him. So, the next morning I dropped my baby off at the sitter but because he knew where I worked, he came there and made a scene telling everyone how many kids I had and how many baby daddies I had. The thing about it is how could you do that, and you also have a child with me and try to chase me all over the country because I decide to move on with my life. Remember this man is already married and has many affairs between me and his wife. So, I was walking by him and he said he wanted to talk to me. I told him I am going to clock in and come back knowing I did not want to see him, so I went inside and did not go back and he cursed me even now. At that time, I was the top salesperson, everyone was looking at me and they knew my name, so my supervisor had to go out and tell him if he didn't leave, she was going to call the police. When I left that day, I was too ashamed to go back to that job until they called me to come back to work and not to worry about him.

In Hindsight

This was hard for me because there was no one to help me and let me know about real love and at the time I thought that was love. I think everyone has a choice no matter what happens in our life, how rough our past has been but for me, I choose to do the thing I knew was wrong. Following my own convictions, but as a sinner, as a person who has been hurt. And being honest, some of the hurt, I cause myself. Coming to the realization I don't have to live out what I had been through as a child.

I didn't stop and concluded there would be conflict in every relationship, in every marriage, but if I kept running, I would have to go through that same cycle over and over. Eventually, I do realize that what my mother endured, the physical and verbal abuse, and we as children had to live through it does not give me the right to hurt others by my actions but as I stated earlier hurting people will always hurt people unless we get help.

I overlooked a lot of good advice from people but at the time I didn't want to hear any of it because my heart wasn't in the right posture to receive any advice. My heart was not transformed as of yet. I wanted to do what I wanted to do and that's it. I became immune to pain and anything else associated with hurt, but I believe that God has an appointed and a set time for everything in our lives and no matter what and how long it takes when that set time comes, we cannot escape it no matter how we try. Don't let the pain or abuse whether it's physically, mentally, or emotionally change the beautiful person you are on the inside because when you are ugly on the inside it will show on the outside so be beautiful inside and outside no matter what life throws at you.

My mom did not like the relationship I had; she knew it was wrong, I had a choice to make. I was tired of the broken men who loved me, at the time love could not pay the bills or help me with my children, this man sent me back to school and the sky was the limit. I love the life of feeling free to do what I wanted financially but when I wanted freedom, it was not really freedom when you are in sin. I love the Lord and hold on to Psalms 23: every day. (A Psalm of David. The Lord is my shepherd; I shall not want. He maketh me to lie down in green pastures: he leadeth me beside the still waters. He restores my soul; He leads me in the paths of righteousness For His name's sake. Yea, though I walk through the valley of the shadow of death, I will fear no evil; For You are with me; Your rod and Your staff, they comfort me. You prepare a table before me in the presence of my enemies; You anoint my head with oil; My cup runs over. Surely goodness and mercy shall follow me All the days of my life; And I will [d]dwell in the house of the LORD Forever. I would read the bible and would even talk with God, but sin was sweet, and the enemy was setting me up for the kill, but God rescued me.

One thing I know is God will rescue us when we want to be rescued, we don't have to say things out loud for others to hear but God pondereth the heart (Prov: 21: 2) and he knew that even though I was in my mess I really wanted to change like a lot of us. None of us wants to stay or keep doing things that are not right. At some point, it will break open and the real truth, as well as revelations, will start to appear.

Understand we always know what's right and what's wrong, so we have to come to the first step of acceptance and owning up to the fact that I am guilty of adultery and want to change but I wasn't ready to change. My heart was not yet turned but it took a word from my son through another person to have that conviction and I did not stop right away. It went on for a couple more years and like the prodigal son I came to myself (Luke 15:17) the change can only come when you come to yourself, in other words, you get sick and tired of being sick and tired of yourself.

Better Days Than Nights

BROWN: Tears and Sadness / BRIGHT RED: Represent Action

Finally moved and secure, he realized he couldn't come to my job anymore and that upset him. He got a vehicle I did not recognize and decided to trail me. While driving to pick up my baby I was looking through my mirror and I saw this car trailing me. When I reach the gas station, I turn in suddenly to make it very obvious if he pulls in too and would get the attention of other people around us.

Since he knew where the sitter was, he went and parked in one of the yards but what he did not know is that I saw him, so I picked up my baby and passed him. I made a quick U-turn going the opposite direction and he didn't see me passing on the other side he was focused on me going a particular way. When I turned off to try to get away from him, I realized I was behind him, so I used my cellphone to call him and said, "How are you trailing me and now I am trailing you?" He said, "I want to talk to you."

Remember, not one time did he ask to see his child. I knew he did not care about our baby when it became clear to him that our relationship was over, he wanted to be spiteful and told me to get the baby ready, he was taking him to do a DNA test. I got the baby ready and when he came back, he told me the lady asked him what he wanted, and he told her he wanted to do a DNA test and the lady looked at him then looked at the baby and laughed. I can only imagine the lady saying to herself, "Since he has money to waste, she will do it."

Back to the story where I am trailing him and he is still trying to talk to me after all he did to me, I did not understand what he wanted. This man swung his car at me knowing I had the baby in the car, so I drove off and while driving I called 911 and pulled into a gas station. Some guys were there in a convertible Mercedes Benz, and they asked me what happened but as they heard the police sirens they drove away, and my baby daddy number five drove away too but turned back because he knew they would go after him.

When the police asked me what happened I told them he was following me trying to see where I lived because I moved in fear of my life. They ask him if he lives in America, and he told them no he does business here and they gave me their card in front of him and said if I ever see him near me, I must call them and they told him that if I call they would put him out the country and he won't be able to come back to America. After all that you would think he would stop. No, now he has a private detective following me like I am some kind of criminal.
Happy to find out my job was closing down at AT&T and I was transferred to Direct TV. Certain in my mind that the

detectives do not know where to find me, wrong again. On one of the phone calls, he quoted my address to let me know he knew where I lived. I could not hide but at least he stayed far enough away from fear of the police. The man never stopped calling me and I would not answer, it was exhausting as he would call not to see the baby, but to try and talk to me. The constant tracking, he would do on my every move had me feeling like a prisoner. Tracking how long it would take me to drive from one place to another and calling me as soon as he thought I had made it home.

A couple of years passed, and things calmed down for a bit, my son was almost two. I started to talk to him and allow him to see his son until one day he told me he wanted to take my son with him to Jamaica for two weeks. Even though it was hard for me to allow that, I really needed a little break. I figured what's the worst that can happen. He won't harm him, it's his son, but little did I know he wanted to use the baby as a pawn to get me back to Jamaica.

I had no intention of going back to that adulterous life, when I was done, I was done. We would talk but that was it. He was starting to realize I wasn't coming back, and my other children were there too with him in Jamaica. He tried to get close to them because if he can't get to me my children were the closest way to get my attention.

My oldest son started to go to the business place where he saw his baby brother and tried to tell my baby daddy number five: I have to say it like that, so I don't have to use names. My son and he had some kind of argument but prior to that, I told my son it's ok son, you can't fight this for me he's got the money and the power so leave it alone.

Next thing I know I called my son. His grandmother told me she does not know where my son is. She told me that she heard that my son, who is my firstborn and my baby daddy had something going on. I was not aware of anything and did not know what she was talking about. Obviously, I started calling my baby daddy trying to find out what was going on and could not get an answer. The next thing I know is my son was dead and I was being told the police killed him. I know there was no reason for the police to kill him and no one would give me details. It took me years to find out his throat was cut.

My son is dead, and I can't go to his funeral in Jamaica because I would be dead too. This man could not touch me as long as I was in America, so he took the baby to Jamaica knowing I love my children with all my heart. He thought he could get me to come so that's how the tough love came in. I had to dig deep in my heart and get tough to save my other children.

I had to let him keep my baby in Jamaica. I can't go to my son's funeral and have to find a way to get my other children here before he kills any more of them. Thank God one of my sons already had his visa so it was easy for him to come. My other son I had to pay thousands of dollars to get him and my daughter. Well, we didn't really see eye to eye at that time, so it took a long time for her to come but

God protected her from him. I tried to get my paperwork in order and put my kids on file but every time he found out what I was doing he would somehow find the people helping me, pay them off so they would mess up my efforts.

Here I am, my children are here illegally, all of us except the baby who was born here. The documents had expired, and I didn't have anything in order, the Lord kept us even though at that time I wasn't saved but I believed in God.

Things started to work out little by little with a great deal of struggle, but God kept us. Until this day I have not come face to face with him and still have not gone back to Jamaica. The memories are still very present. God has not released me of them yet because I know God will save that man's life, so my baby son who is now a teenager says he never wants to go back to Jamaica.

Things got really tough as I didn't see my baby again until he was almost six and the reason why was because his dad had to take him back to America. I would not sign the papers when my son's passport expired and even though he had multiple businesses in Jamaica he was British so I am the mother and Jamaican so I am the only one who could get my child dual nationality in Jamaica and so he had to bring my child back to me.

My brother in Florida picked up my child because I did not want to see him after taking my child, not even taking him to his house but he gave my child to one of his women to raise him and they told him I was dead while he would come here to America watching me and chasing me all over the country.

I moved so many times and broke so many leases and the last place I stopped was Philadelphia. I decided I was done running from this man who wanted to kill me for leaving him. I had to be safe now and my family was in Philadelphia but my big sister who is my half-sister and her husband always stayed in touch with my child's father, the same baby daddy number five. I was so angry at them, how they could know that my child's father is trying to kill me, and they want to be his best friend.

My brother in Florida took my son and kept him for me until we could find out how to get my youngest son to me without my child's father knowing how and when he was coming. My brother had a daughter just a couple of months older than my son and one day they were playing and for some reason, my little niece picked up my son's shoes and to their amazement, the bottom of the shoes could open and when my little niece showed it to her dad my brother, he found a piece of paper with some information written on it like a credit card information.

While my son was with my brother he told my son, his nephew that he is going to take him to see his mother, but my son said my mother is dead as that is what the women told him in Jamaica. My brother told him no, your mother is not dead, she is in Jamaica. My brother convinces him, and I started to remind my son about some things, but he was too young to remember, anyway my brother and I decided to dump everything his dad brought because we didn't know what else he had hidden in the teddy bear and his other stuff so I told my brother not to send any of that stuff. Just dump everything. We also started to use text to communicate just in case any bug was in the stuff. I told my brother the flight information via text and paid the extra for the flight attendant to take care of him on the flight. I told my brother to buy him one outfit only and send him to me because I already have everything for him. By this time, I was saved, sanctified, and filled with the Holy Ghost. God is fighting this battle now; he was always fighting the battle for me but I needed to be equipped with the Holy Spirit and know it.

Just before my son came back to America the Lord put me on a twenty-one day fast and at the end of that fast the Lord told me to extend my fast three more days and at the end of the fast that's when I got the call that my son was in Florida waiting for me to pick him up. God had already told me what to expect when my son comes to me. The time has come for me to pick him up, my almost six-year-old son from the airport whom I hadn't seen since he was one and a half, so I am at the airport waiting for the flight attendant with my ID to pick up my son but it's almost like when he saw me, he had an instant connection with me. I started to talk with him and ask him what kind of toys he liked. He told me so I told him we are going to the store to get him a toy, I asked him if he was hungry he said yes so while we were going to get him something to eat I started to ask him if he remembers me as his mother and he said no. I got him something to eat first and just couldn't believe that my little baby boy was back home with me.

He was like a little man, you can tell he was well trained, his dad is very big on education so he got a great start, so after getting him food and his toy we headed home and when we got home I started to show him all the stuff I bought for him and also took out old pictures of him as a baby with me and him and he looked at the pictures and smiled. I began to show him that I still have all his stuff and he was amazed.

He was so good with numbers when we went to church, and they would always pick on him to come read a lesson. The elders in the church would give him money because they were amazed at his level of intelligence for his age so I can give his dad credit for that. He was very big on education, so now my baby son is here with me and now his dad is calling me wanting to know where I live and wants to come and visit his child.

He will never know where I live because I already know it's not really about the child, he just wants to get close to me, but I would not under any circumstances tell him or invite him where I live. This man has no shame, you would think that a man with his status would just take his money and find someone else. Not that he doesn't have anybody he just knows they all just want money, and I was there to help him build his business. I walked away from everything because what I am learning in my walk with Christ is that everything, we gain in life that God didn't give us, he strips

29

us of everything and gives us what he wants, everything the devil gave us has to go when we surrender to Christ.

I have a relationship with Christ now because it took until I was sick and tired of being sick and tired to get my attention and that was the best thing I have ever done, not that there are no obstacles or challenges but because the Lord is with me. It allows me to handle every situation that comes my way knowing that the Lord is with me every step of the way.

In Hindsight

There were many tears, and they came from my pain and all that I went through that took me to this point. The tears are really about regrets, hurts, guilt, and shame. I thank God for them too as where would I be without them?

When you find yourself in a situation, don't just try to handle it on your own, find someone who you can trust to talk to because the pain is real. When we are in pain the first thing that looks like comfort to us, we will gravitate to but only to find out that very thing is the thing that will or is going to inflict more pain. The pain will be greater than the first so please don't settle for more pain and remember that Jesus said, "The thief comes only to steal and to kill and destroy, I came that they may have life, and have it abundantly." John: 10:10.

Don't allow the devil to steal anything else from you when you already lost whatever you lost. Seek help and don`t look for love in the wrong places. The pain is real but so is the healing. The grieving process while painful is healing.

My actions were out of pain and lack of love, I was wounded and did not even know it. I had no one to tell me this because everyone around me was wounded. We just didn't know we were all wounded. We dress up all our wounds until one day the band aid starts to fall off and only then do, we realize we had a full-blown sore underneath and didn't know. Don't put the band aid on the wound, every now and then you have to lift that band aid and see if that wound is getting better.

My inside wanted freedom but I had a mask on the outside so no one could see beyond the mask but now I am so glad for Jesus. He is merciful and forgiving and his blood has redeemed me from the curse of sin, shame, and condemnation. Now I am walking in liberty because who the Son set free is free indeed. John 8:36.

So always ask yourself, are you doing the best you can? Or is someone else allowing you to do what they think is best and know there is a difference. Send yourself through a process of discovery and find the truth even if it hurts to know it may have been hurting you.

Head Over Heels in Love- Not

RED: Life-Changing / GREEN: Growth and Strength

I have cried myself to sleep many times after coming to Christ. The reason is, it's not easy coming from the world of doing what I wanted to do and no convictions. After I surrender my life to Christ, I have to do what God wants me to do and I did not have all my I's and T's crossed but one thing for sure, I love Jesus and I try to do everything I can to not get out of the will of God.

I know while I am on this journey with Christ my Son whom I just got back from his dad and now he does not want anything to do with his dad. I was telling him to forgive his dad or that is what was coming out of my words, but I was struggling to forgive him at that time myself. I know my son needed a male figure in his life and he won't open up about what he had gone through while he was taken away, I knew it was too hard on him.

One day I was talking about my firstborn son who was killed. It was obvious that he knew his father had information about the killing. He overheard them talking about it. He figured out his dad caused his brother's death. The more he thought about it the more he became angry and now he really didn't want to talk to his dad at all. I felt really bad because he wasn't supposed to hear any of that and there was nothing I could do to change that, so I just continue to encourage him. Telling him no matter what he must forgive his dad or Jesus won't forgive him of his sins.

I had a tough time adjusting to having my little son and all the responsibilities of caring for a child. I would have to work, take him to school, pick him up from school by a certain time, and go to church. I had no one to help because as I mentioned my family and I aren't on speaking terms. There was so much interference in my business, and they were so focused on my life instead of their own, I just didn't trust them. I did not feel comfortable telling them where I lived because they were still talking to my baby`s father who was trying to kill me.

Even on trips, they made to Jamaica he would go where my family was to look for them and I just couldn't understand why they would do that. No matter how much I dislike someone for whatever reason and the family knows someone wants to hurt you, why is this even an issue? Why do you even want to be around a family that is not supporting you? You would think the family would come first. I was asked, "What did I do to deserve all that?" and I would say, "Nothing that I know about because no one has ever said anything." At one point I felt like I was from a different dad and that was not so. My mother was married to my dad, and we all grew up with a mother and a father. Despite all the physical abuse my dad did to my mother and us; sometimes being beaten just because my dad was drunk.

More family matters, my sister is the one who my mother had before she met my dad. No matter how I tried to show love to my sister there is always something, so we never stayed in a good relationship for long. There was blame put on me if her husband was looking at me inappropriately, and I would try to tell her what I saw in him, but those discussions backfired on me too. Let me just say to the ladies and even gentlemen, if you see someone who is acting in a way and then pretends, they are not, then look in the mirror and stop lying to yourself.

I have been accused of many things by my family, most of which I don't have a clue and the problem is they never come and say anything directly to me so I just live and learn to love them from a distance and whenever I can bless them. I still do with a pure heart because I will never give people's words power over me. After all, God knows it all so I learned that it's just me and my kids and they will grow to see things even if I didn't have to tell them.

As the years go by, being saved and still trying to go through life with God leading me every step of the way, had some bumps in the road. In church, I went to God with my mind made up and in spite of all that the enemy tried to throw at me, I never lost my faith in God. Years later I met a man I thought was the one, but truth be told he was wounded and did not want to be helped. He had too much pride and also, he knew he was not right, so he didn't want to be exposed. No one can hide from the Holy Ghost for long. When God is ready to reveal stuff, we can't stop it.

I was so happy that my son would have a dad in his life that I missed all the signs God was showing me in the beginning because I was distracted with what I wanted and not God's perfect will for my life. I settled with God's permissive will and I created "Ishmael" and had to live with "Ishmael" until God delivered me. "Ishmael" is not his name but there is a story about Sarah and Abraham in Genesis where Sarah went against God's will and created "Ismael."

I was crying for God to help me. I married based on my will instead of God's will and even though the marriage was done the way God said to do it, it wasn't God's perfect will for my life. This man didn't want God, he just wanted God until he married me, and I didn't make it easy for him with my mouth.

I asked God if you want one soul, or you don't want any soul because if I stay in this marriage, you won't get any soul. God did not deliver me because I was uncomfortable in the marriage but there was infidelity in a marriage that was supposed to be Godly. My ex-husband left us a couple of times, some of which I told him to leave. He had another house that he could run to, so he did not hesitate at any time because he knew what he was doing and, on many occasions, I asked him to get rid of that house and he did not want to. He wanted another place he could go to and every time I would take him back my son would tell me, mom, why do you keep taking dad back? Over that period of time, he started to call my ex-husband dad, so I told him son I am a child of God and I am waiting for the Lord to release me from this marriage. I can't do what everyone else does and I know his little heart was broken. It brought back a memory of when we had just got married and my son's school would have parent-teacher meetings and we would both go and at the end of the meeting he would hold both of our hands and smiling when we are walking out to the car. He was so happy for his friends to see he has a mom and a dad even though he didn't say it, I could tell what his little heart was saying, and I really held on for a long time.

After adultery, if only one person wants to fix a relationship or a marriage it will never work out. We have to first acknowledge that we have a fault and then pray and ask God to help us, but it can't be a one-sided thing. When a husband or a wife brings in an outsider and goes as far as going into your cell phone, taking out the "wife" as programed in the phone, and replacing it with her given name "Diane", she wants the wife to know that she is out there. All this lying and everything else and I am not saying I was innocent, my mouth was doing a lot, and the fact that he tried to make me look stupid by telling me the phone did that on its own. I had to let him know the phone might be a smartphone but it's not so smart to replace your wife's name with the girlfriend's name and then do the same thing with my son.

In Hindsight

The way I felt about all of this was no sin goes unpunished, Prov:11:21 and whatever we sow we will reap, no matter how much God loves us we will pay for our actions. I am not saying my ex-husbands were doing what God wanted them to do but when it happened, I got a taste of my own medicine. Whatever we do, it will come back one way or another now or later, when we come to Christ after all our sinful ways, he forgives us, but we have to pay for our sins. The penalty may not be as severe as when we were still in sin, but God does not alter his word because we got saved.

I see myself now speaking, especially to ladies young and old and even men sharing my testimony. Traveling from country to country doing what God has called me to do, writing my story, sharing everything that I have gone through and will ever go through, telling them about the love of Jesus and how he saved me from the pits of hell.

Well, I had no way of knowing how or even when things would turn around for me but one thing, I know for certain is I have fallen in love with Jesus. He is there and will catch me before I fall so, I put total trust and confidence in him knowing that at my appointed time my change will come and know that God will turn everything around and cause them to work for my good and his glory. Romans: 8:28.

Words of confirmation, dreams, visions, and the way things are lining up in my life, sometimes when the Lord show us by way of these gifts or even prophecy be careful not to get weary in well doing Galatians: 6:9 because God's word will never look like what we think it should look like and if we are not careful we can miss God by assuming how and what the blessing should look like. Believe me, everything in this book is from my own experience, don't miss God by your own perception.

The Saving Grace

Gold – Glory, Grace & Divinity

The breaking point that led me to Christ was when I found myself at a low place in my life. Going through heartbreak in my relationship, it was that moment I could feel a drawing and a sense of surrender not realizing at that time, it was God drawing me to him. After my ex had broken my heart and was trying to win me back, we had planned a trip to Florida on Memorial Day. There was some mismatch in our schedule my ex went ahead, and my brother and I were going to meet him there. I noticed that all that Friday night my spirit was in agony, well at the time I didn't know what I was feeling. My ex realized I did not call him, and I had missed my flight so he called me, and I answered the phone but there was nothing he could do to get me to come to Florida. My mind was changed and there was nothing he could do or say to make me come to Florida. He told me he would pay the difference on the flight that I missed, and he was going to rest. I was supposed to call him when I landed in Florida but little did he know I was under Holy Ghost arrest. I did not know what it was either, I just knew not to go where he was.

I had a burning desire to go to church so that same weekend I got dressed and went to church and I couldn't wait for the altar call. While at the altar giving my life to Christ, I was crying I saw a presence overshadowing me. All of this was new to me, and it took a couple of hours of me being at the altar. I had to make a decision to walk away from the man I thought I loved. During those times the mothers of the church would tarry with you until you get your breakthrough. It ended up being a four-hour experience. The feeling of love came over me that I have never felt before and it was then that I knew in my heart that I was not to live without that feeling again.

It may have taken me hours, but I surrendered to Christ and chose Jesus. The role of my ex was quickly put into perspective. I chose life over death. A life lived in Christ is life and a life living in sin is death and that's how my journey with Christ began. No looking back ever since. Of course, I had bumps along the road but the journey with Jesus kept me aligned.

In Hindsight

I heard what God was trying to tell me and I began to follow his lead. I stopped adding my own definitions to what God was doing in my life and let him be the teacher.

The Real Thing (God)

PURPLE - Transformation / GREEN - Growth & Strength
RAINBOW – Revelation/ ORANGE - Transition

Well, it's true when the Lord tells us no sin will go
unpunished Proverbs:11:21. ("*Though* hand *join* in hand,
the wicked shall not be unpunished: but the seed of the
righteous shall be delivered.") For years I was the other
woman and now it is my turn to be on the other end.
Though God may save us from our past sins that does not
mean that when we come to Christ we won't go through
times of confusion or challenges. The problem I had was
not that I couldn't stay and forgive my husband but there
was no remorse on his part. He acted as if I was the one
who committed adultery, so he did not help to work things
out either. There was too much pride involved. I don't want
anyone in my business, I waited until God gave me the go-
ahead to get the divorce.

While going through in my marriage God was using the
situation in my marriage to show me about myself that even
though I thought I was saved and sanctified, I had stuff in
me that I was not delivered from. I always say that
experience was my practice marriage (smile). I had to wait
it out until God deliver me from that marriage. He didn't
want the divorce, but he wasn't willing to do the work
either. He thought we could be married and live in the

same house in separate rooms, I told him if I wanted a roommate, I would not have to marry anyone to get a roommate.

When I married, I didn't marry to get a break from my husband, and he got a break from me. I understand sometimes we may lay in a different room, but the matrimonial bed is where we should sleep. I may be old-fashioned, but I understand never to give place to the devil. So before and after the divorce, I didn't like him, and he didn't like me. I told the Lord how I feel and that I don't want to pray for him but after a while, my heart started to get soft. I couldn't stay there but little do we know that we never really know what we are capable of until we are put to the test.

When the Lord said, "The heart is deceitfully wicked." believe it (Jerimiah: 17: 9-10). God's word is true and if you don't know it and haven't been there, keep living. I had to repent to God first because I know better, and my actions were not lining up with my words. After a while, I had to call him and tell him that I was sorry. We both apologize for each part we played in our marriage, and I can say that the Lord has brought us to a good place with each other. We can say hello to each other every now and then and I see God has used him in my life in a mighty way.

After the divorce, God gave me favor with him and I think if I had not hurried up and forgiven him what God did would not have worked out so well. I learn no matter what, it can be hard at times but let the Lord fight our battle

Psalms: 46:10. ("Be still and know that I *am* God: I will be exalted among the heathen, I will be exalted in the earth.") God has brought me a mighty long way, from running away from any man that sounded like my dad, any man who thinks I would allow them to treat me any kind of way, to God humbling me, to stop running and trust him (God) to show me how to stay even when it gets uncomfortable. God showed me how to forgive my husband who cheated on me even though we got a divorce, not because of me but because he didn't want it bad enough and God would not let me stay in something that is one-sided. He had his chances to get it right but as I said, "He didn't want it bad enough."

God called me and had work for me to do so God is not going to allow anyone to mess up his plan. I must move on and be about God's business. I have been doing what God has called me to do, well not everything but as I go, he makes things clearer to me so now I am going step by step as the Lord leads. I am going on in my single life, my children are trying to do their best to be happy and make me happy.

The family event I want to mention is one of my sons, my 4th son, who went down a new road got locked up. This was his first time being incarcerated however subsequently it happened three times back-to-back. Someone threatened him and he decided to carry a gun and was pulled over with it, but I know God was protecting him because there was a "calling" against his life. I used these words because he is deceased, so during the time he was locked up and I was not familiar with the jail, just knowing that my child was behind bars I would cry every night.

One night the lord asked me why I was crying and showed me that it was him who caused my son to be in jail. It was hard because the police had beaten him, stomp his foot, broke it, and locked him up without taking him to the doctor. I had to call the prison, ask for the warden, and let them know that they may see him as a prisoner, but he is my son, and he is somebody and if they don't take him to the doctor, I was going to bring channel 29 TV station to the prison. My son was in pain, and they were acting like he was nobody so they eventually took him to the doctor so they could look at his foot and treat him like a real person.

I never cried again until long after when I went to the prison, and it was obvious that I don't know anything about what do to when you visit someone in jail so I would go there and would have to take off all my jewelry and they have to search me as if I am a prisoner too. As time goes by the Lord has given me the strength to go through the process with my son, I had to visit him in the rain, the sun, and the snow. One day he said, "Mom, why is it you never wear your nice jewelry?" I said to him, "Son they strip me before I come back here." He hung his head down because he knows I am not used to that kind of treatment. He himself was not used to prison but that was my Moses on the backside of the mountain only that was his mountain, prison.

It was time to get ready for court. I had to get a lawyer for him and when the case was tried and he was sentenced, God showed him favor. He was complaining the lawyer could do better after God had reduced his sentence. The policeman wanted to put him away for a long time saying he assaulted him. Six of those police officers were holding him and beating him so the Judge told the policeman he is throwing out the case. What they didn't realize was that the Holy Ghost showed up when I showed up and God won't let them put anything else on him especially if it was a lie. His sentence was one and a half to three years, he got out in a year. During that time, he was saying the lawyer could get him less time and the Lord spoke to him and asked him why he was complaining about the punishment of his crime? He had to spend a year and a half but had to spend the time waiting on trial. Lamentation 3:38-40 "Is it not from the mouth of the Most High That woe and well-being proceed? Why should a living man complain, A man for the punishment of his sins? Let us search out and examine our ways and turn back to the LORD."

The time he spent wasn't easy for him or me but with God's help, we got through it. Finally, he served the time and the Judge granted him his freedom to come home. While he was in prison, he was reading the word, talking to the other prisoners about Jesus and while he was there, he didn't get all his stuff together, meaning paperwork so God gave him favor and the ICE Immigration Judge paid the fees.

He got out on Valentine's Day 2019 and later was diagnosed with stage three cancer on Valentine's Day of

2020. He went through the whole process of chemotherapy and radiation. Before he started all the treatments, he had no insurance, and the hospital would not look after him, so he was in pain for a couple of months and cancer started to spread in his body.

One day the Lord put me on a three-day fast and sent me to Philadelphia to lay my hands on him, put my prayer shawl around him, and pray for him. My son did not want me to see him like that and his brother was watching him go through it all as they both lived in the same house. That's son number three. Sons number three and four always lived together and are best friends.

I remember that and I cried because I was feeling his pain. I went on the three-day fast as God had instructed me, went to their house, prayed, laid my hands on him, and left. My son was going through a lot of pain and finally, after months of seeing him suffering, he had been approved for insurance and could now go in for surgery to remove this cancer, start chemotherapy, then radiation. My son got through all that with God's grace, mercy and came out healed. He starting to gain back his weight and he called me so happy to see his hair growing back. We would get on video so he could show me his hairline growing back and he was looking so good. God had transformed him better than he was before he was diagnosed with cancer.

On the fourth of July, my 3rd son wanted to pick me and their little brothers up in Maryland and spend time with the family. I really wanted to drive so I asked him to just let me drive. He was just feeling that he should just come and pick us up, so he did. Not knowing that time would be the last days I got to spend with him and my 4th son.

We had a great time with the food, family, and friends. That evening while we were outside, he got ready and was going out on the road, so he came to tell me he was leaving but when I looked at him, I asked God in my spirit, "God what are you getting ready to do, are you fixing him up to take him?" I just felt in my spirit that my son was looking so good, and I felt that God had healed him and fixed him up to take him home. I spent the day after July fourth at my friend's house and then was picked up by my 4th son, who is deceased, the next day to return to their home in Philadelphia. While driving, I was thinking that I have never driven with him before so even now I was doing things for the first time. When we were ready to leave back to Maryland, he came out to help put my stuff in the car not knowing that would be the last time I saw him. Prior to that I realize that a couple of months before I found myself wearing all black and I asked the Lord, "Who am I going to mourn and why am I wearing all this black?"

In the prayer ministry, God gave me a minister who told everyone online to give me one hundred dollars each and that I will know what to do with the money, so God was helping me with money for my son's funeral. The Lord had been preparing me for it all along. In August he got his result from his check-up, it was a Thursday and there was no more cancer in his body. He didn't get a chance to tell me, he only told me before that his covid-19 test was negative. He didn't get a chance to share the good news with me, that same Saturday someone shot him in his back and told us they thought it was someone else. When the shooter found out who it was, they shot, he then killed himself, or that's what they say happened.

My son who survived so much, who fought back everything that was fighting him is gone. Survived cancer only for God to take him home but we witnessed God's power of healing in a powerful way. God's restoration in my son's body, God's love demonstrated through him in a mighty way and he was just loving everyone telling everyone about Jesus before the Lord took him. One thing I learned, God does not work or do things the way we expect. He is bigger and does things in a way we may never completely understand.

Times can really get hard for us because he was healed, looking better than before, he was cancer-free, and he was gone. His brother/roommate took it really hard since they were always together. People were calling me crying and the Lord would have me consoling them when they realize they should be comforting me. All of a sudden, they would stop crying and some were afraid to call me. When they did call, they were in amazement at how strong I was. God gave me supernatural strength and would not let me cry. God said, "In the face of my enemy remember God knows who our enemies are, they don't always have a pitchfork and red horns."

My son had two children and was married but it did not look like everyone was on good terms so because they were still married, I had to get together with her, her mother, and my other son to get his body. We also had to be in agreement with the burial spot we all agreed on. I was the one preparing everything. I think God gave me supernatural strength even now after a year, still fresh, so we made the arrangements for the whole funeral, wake and repass. And by this, his sister was here my only daughter who I had not seen in about 20 years.

If you think that God does some strange things to us but for God, it all has a purpose. The Lord told me to sing at the funeral. I had to stand over my son's dead body and sing hallelujah my God reign and almost preached at the funeral. God did not allow me to stop anything during that time, I was ministering online all the times I was supposed to. When we are going through things that don't mean God's work is stopped. THE LORD TOLD ME, "WHEN THE MANGO IS RIPE YOU DON'T LEAVE IT ON THE TREE TO ROT YOU PICK IT." In other words, my son was ripe for the picking. Keeping him in earthly matters would only make things worse. God knew where he belonged.

I told you, in the beginning, I had five kids and the Lord took two of my sons, well they were not really mine they really belonged to God, he just lent them to me. When my first son died, which he was really the first one by birth, I wasn't saved. That grieving period was different. Now I am in Christ it's a total difference. The pain is the same, but the grieving is different. God allows me to keep going, as I have to live and fulfill my God-given assignment and I still have three more children which are going through a hard time. I have to say to God, "You give me such hard cases."

My baby which is now a teenager never speaks about anything. He remembers his dad took him away when he was almost two and when I got him back, he was six thinking that I was dead. That was hard having him back and having to train his brain to know that I am really his mom and not the woman his dad told him was his mother. Now he has to deal with the loss of having two brothers killed. One he only heard about but the other he was there to see after spending time fourth of July 2020. He hung out in his brother's room with him the whole time we were in Philadelphia and that was the last time he sees his brother, so he just shuts down. You can't get anything out of him. I told him if he wants to go for counseling, we can go but he says he is good and now all he wants is to smoke weed, or I should say marijuana. He hardly ever eats and really acts as if he doesn't care about anything. Now it's not easy for me to know my son is in pain but won`t let me help him. His older brother calls and tries to talk to him but he himself is grieving, he can't even look at his niece and nephew because they really look like their dad.

It's not easy for my older son to be around them and my daughter is in another state, and she was close to her brother as well. She doesn't want to be around anything to remind her about her brother. None of them can handle it so I have to suck it up as the Lord has graced me to go through this grieving process in his strength. I can hold up my children and my grandchildren with his help.

I have never lost my praise in spite of everything I have been and still going through, God is still my refuge and my strength through it all, and don`t get me wrong, I would be lying if I said I did not have moments of weakness but that's when his strength has made me strong. I have been through the fire and been through the flood, but nothing can stop me from praising my God.

I remember before I got saved, I was in a relationship and after I got saved and realize I had to give up all the worldly pleasures and the man I have really loved. At least I thought I loved until I learned that I didn't know what love really was until I met Jesus.

We were just two broken people trying to find love. I know now that hurting people only know how to hurt people so don't go into a relationship broken and looking for someone to make you whole or happy. God is the only one who can mend our brokenness. I realize that no matter what we do or try to do until we surrender our life and our entire being to God, we will always be struggling in one way or another. Let me tell you that again when we have issues being in Christ it will work out much better than trying to do it in our own strength. Any issue I might add.

I remember when I got saved as I was telling God to allow me to get what I needed out of my system, and it wasn't a long time because he had work for me to do. My ex had committed to changing his car and when he changes his car, he then got me a new vehicle too. After I got saved, I did not want any residue from my past in my relationship with God. When you fall in love with the one and only JESUS you don't want anything in the way. I got rid of furniture everything else that was a reminder of my past. I would always ask Jesus to please get me out of this vehicle that is a memory of my ex, even though I still owed money on it. Not to mention the vehicle almost killed me three times. The third time was because of my disobedience. I almost died on the New Jersey Turnpike when God told me not to go to New York to a funeral but my brother whom I love so much wanted me to come. I disobeyed God for my brother and though God worked it out for my good, I was disobedient. God used that accident to get me out of that vehicle, the one I had been praying for him to take me out of for the longest time.

The vehicle was crushed from back to front, and I came out without a scratch. Owing on the vehicle God still gave me favor and got me out of the vehicle and got me into a better vehicle. Ever since then any vehicle I ever bought, God always picked them out and I had someone who I use to work for co-sign.

While purchasing the new vehicle, I received instructions from God to give to the co-signer. I told them they should pay for the vehicle and let me pay them instead of the bank. They told me they would think about it however they did not agree. Months after I was released from my job and when I could not make the payment, they were upset with me. God already knew what was going to happen and since they rejected the word God, he let them pay off the vehicle, sent the title to me in my name, and I got a check for the balance because the vehicle was paid off before the time so in my disobedience, God still worked it out and it`s not because God changed his mind or his word but there was a testimony to come from that so I never tried to be disobedient again. After that vehicle was paid off God has never allowed me to owe money on any vehicle. All the vehicles since then he gave me, and I never owed anything. I always have the title in my hands. God is truly amazing.

If you ask me if I ever do not listen, well no, sometimes but I still get it wrong. I do believe when our hearts are in the right posture whatever happens at that moment God can use our mess to make a great message.

Now I said earlier in the book that I got married seven years after serving God to a man who was broken, and I was a work in progress, but he wanted me more than he wanted Jesus and I had a problem with that. I thought I was his savior, and I was trying to do God`s job for him as if God needed my help, Lol.

I Love God and believe in him because he had shown me so many miracles in my life. I know God is who he says he is, but I wanted my ex-husband to know that too, but he had a different agenda. He didn't want that because he had too many people telling him that he could play around in church then marry me. He thought he wouldn't be exposed but God has invested too much in me to allow me to stay in that mess.

He was trying to kill me, but he realizes that greater is he who lives inside of me. Everything he tried he was exposed, and he then hated me as much as I hated him but what I realize is that God was using all that to prune me, to mold me, and to make me. I ask the Lord to release me and even though it took a while God uses everything for his good and for his glory. We had been married for almost eight years and out of those eight years, we only lived together for one full year. He would always get a text message, then leave for the other house that he insisted on keeping. There was no consideration to selling it or renting it out either. At this point, I would make it easy for him since that is what he wanted to do. Go, the lies and cheating were too much for me to forget. I always say, "you don't have to lie if you don't have anything to hide."

No romance, still married, and thank God the Holy Spirit started to show me all the insights and what was happening in the marriage. We could not be free in intimacy because I kept to myself. I was saved and refuse to let him interrupt my peace and come with all the nonsense he was doing. I would not forgive him, and he had no remorse, he acted like nothing was wrong and he did not want to get help either. I went for counseling, but he did not want to go so when enough becomes enough God released me.

Now I am focusing on God and would like to be married again but waiting for God to send me a husband who will love him (God) first then me. My ex-husband and I did not speak but God had done some amazing things and had used him to do what he did not do while we were married. God used him to bless me beyond my wildest imagination and he is not even sure why. Once alimony payments were complete, he still found himself paying. God is listening, and take it from me, God will not allow anyone to take advantage of his children. All we have to do is follow God's ways. I did not say be perfect but follow God's way and not render evil for evil. When you do that, it looks like the enemy is winning but all we have to do is hold our peace and watch God.

In Hindsight:

I am stronger now than before, whatever the devil thought would kill me, God made it my steppingstone. No matter what comes my way now, I think I was BUILT TO LAST, TESTED, AND APPROVED, BY GOD. The enemy does not know what to do with me as Job mentioned in Job: 13:15. "Thou you slay me yet will I trust you." and as Job:1:21 also says, "Naked I came into this world and naked I will return." Therefore, in all my tests and trials I learn to wear everything loosely.

God gives us everything on this earth not to make idols of them but to know he is the giver of life and everything in between. My life has changed for the better since I accepted Christ. It's one thing to accept Christ but we must have a daily relationship with him, allow him to transform us from the inside out, allow him to teach us, to lead us, and to guide us every step of the way.

Engage The Holy Spirit, I don't do anything without asking his Holy Spirit for help and believe me sometimes I do things and then remember I didn't ask him. It's ok when you remember just say sorry to Holy Spirit and keep moving. Always acknowledge him tell him everything. How you feel and what you don't like, he cares about every little detail of our life.

He told me that years ago when I was getting ready to move and wanted some paper to wrap my glass dishes and other things, I was thinking about where to get that much paper and one morning I went to work and as I went to the trash shoot to throw out some trash, in the middle of the room there was a Macy's bag full of paper. Neatly wrapped, I look at the bag, smiled, looked up, and said, "JESUS YOU GOT JOKES, BUT THANK YOU." It was that moment when the Lord spoke to me and said, "He cares about every little detail of my life."

Trust God with your life, he will do wonders with it. Don't worry, some days are going to be better than others but keep going, don't stop no matter what. The enemy will try to whisper in your ear but remember always give him the Word of God. Find a scripture that works for you and whenever you need that scripture, The Holy Spirit will bring it to your remembrance even if you don't remember it just say, "Jesus." God is an awesome God, and I couldn't see myself living without him even if I wanted to. I know too much about him not to trust him. He has shown me too much so when the Lord reveals himself to us, we have no choice but to trust him.

The New World, So I thought

BLACK: Hardship/ BLUE: Trust

Just when I thought a new world was ahead of me, there comes another situation. I share and share so you can clearly see God in all these situations and how he works with us, for us, and all for the good.

Taking you away from the men in my life, and into my money, right now, I am in a situation with the IRS and it's nothing that I did, but I trusted a family member to do my taxes. I don't know what he did to create this situation however, he is mad with me as if I did something to him. All these years I uses a stranger to do my taxes and did not have a problem. One day he told me he did taxes and I said, "ok." I will give him a try. I referred a lot of people to him, and I am the only one whose taxes were out of order. I told him about it, and he would not fix it. I did what I knew I could do at that time, I cried out to God and prayed for God to forgive him. The funny thing is, he does not talk to me, and I am the one who should be upset. Over time I just surrendered and told him that whatever was done knowingly or unknowingly, I wanted to be forgiven and I forgave him as well. Sometimes we don't realize that people don't have a problem with us it's the spirit in them that can't stand the God in us.

I am still trying to process in general how someone can be so nice in one minute and then just flip to another personality and it is really a spirit using that person to

57

attack us, but we cannot be distracted no matter who it is. We just have to have an ear to hear and eyes to see what the Lord is showing us through all situations.

In Hindsight

There will always be something going on in our lives that may cause us hardship, pain, or sadness however with the love and trust for God you will have everything you need to get through it, you are never alone.

The Words of Wisdom from Christ to Pre-Christ Growth

YELLOW: Wisdom
PURPLE: Transformation / ORANGE: Transition
BLUE: Loyalty & Trust

On the journey with Christ, we have to remember that we are never alone, and we will go through a lot of struggles. It takes time to see the whole picture and we will never see things all at once because it's a step-by-step journey. God will not show us everything at once but as we learn to trust him and to walk by faith, he will keep revealing himself to us.

A very important experience I had was learning that how we respond to situations in our life will determine how much we will grow. We can remain stagnant if we choose but God's desire is for us to move from drinking milk to eating hard food and it took me a while to figure that out. I had to "Go around the mountain." a few times like the children of Israel in Genisis:46:2-4 and Genesis :50:24-25. God never holds us up, we hold God up and he won't move until we do. What he instructed us to do the first time when he reveals it, so obedience is key. Listening and hearing God's voice is also a blessing and will come from you wanting to know God more and more every day.

Don't try to figure God out, it's a step-by-step move. Just trust God and rely on him in every area of your life. Take your will out of the equation completely and allow God's will to rule in our life. We must learn to want what God wants and hate what God hates and when we learn to do that, everything will fall into place. Giving God full control of our lives and he will show us step by step, little by little what the finished product will look like. God can do anything quickly if he desires or chooses but we wouldn't learn anything we would probably think it's us who is in control. You will also learn that God will never share His Glory with anyone, no matter how he loves us. I had to learn quickly that when I trust God and allow Him to lead me and guide me every step of the way I cannot and will not fail. In my life's journey, the Lord can go only where I allow God to take me and it's not easy when we can't see where we are going and that's where faith comes in. "We walk by faith and not by sight." 2 Corinthians: 5:7. It's up to us how eagerly we want the things of God because everything else on this earth is temporary, even life.

The best way to get connected with God is to tap into the source and the only way to tap into the source is to be connected through prayer and fasting, having a relationship with God is key in order to get to know him. You have to get to know him, to know his ways, know what he likes and dislikes. In other words, spend time, earn trust. After spending time with God, he will start to tell you things and show you things. Many things will blow your mind. God is always waiting to have a relationship with you. This is one relationship where you can guarantee you will never get hurt. Everyone will find their way of comfort with God when you have finally surrendered your life to Christ.

What works for me might not necessarily work for you may be singing will be what works for you, maybe helping others is what will work for you, etc., everyone has their own walk with the Lord. I can only tell you my story but as you go along, I promise you God will reveal to you what he wants you to do to build you up from the inside out and embrace it. Things that you don't understand as you go along, ask God or if he connects you with someone that he wants to help you along the way. He will start putting people in your path but just make sure it is a divine connection and you will know because you will feel it in your spirit. God will lead you and guide you, but you must pay attention and don't be distracted as I did at first. There will always be bumps in the roads like anything else but just trust God with it all. "He will make every crooked path straight." Isaiah: 45:2. Just be ready for a life-changing experience. Your life will never be the same. God is about to blow your mind.

Ask me how I know, well I am a living testimony of my own strengths, weaknesses, lessons, and experiences. It's also why I can tell you about my experiences and not that of anyone else. It's important to share what you learn in life with others so they can continue to see that God is the same, God is love.

Getting Started

What the Lord taught me to do in my early walk when I just got saved was to surrender myself to everything that represents God. I didn't want to hear or look at anything that would taint my spirit, not that I am perfect or think I am but even if I wanted to sway, God would not allow me to. He takes away every other taste that was contrary to his and only gives me a taste for his things. I was taught how to dress, how to pray, he taught me everything. Sometimes I wanted to do what I wanted to do but I was and still am so in Love with Jesus. When you fall in love with someone there is no way you want to do anything that would make them leave. Jesus does that in you.

I have grown accustomed to my relationship with Jesus and his presence that I have no desire to live without him. My prayer for years is, "Lord don't let me stumble or fall and if you see me falling, please balance me back up." and he did just that. It's nothing I did on my own, but I think I maintain the right posture before a Holy God and he honored my request.

When you have the Holy Spirit there is no way we can do anything that is wrong without the Holy Spirit convicting us. You see I live a life of repentance even if I don't do anything I live my life every day like I did something. I always would repent day and night for even my thoughts because we have thoughts that we are not even aware of. Our deeds and actions that we are not aware of so if we live a life of repentance every day then the enemy, the accuser of the brethren won't have anything to come at us with. We don't give him an open door to our life because if we leave a door open, he will walk right in. I try my best to be sensitive to the nudging of the Holy Spirit, he is the one who will lead us and guide us when we come to Christ and allow Him to fill us with his Holy Spirit.

The Holy Spirit is very relevant, don't ignore him. He will teach you things no man or woman ever could. We never have to impress God just come as we are and allow a Holy God to do the transformation in our lives. Often, we think we have to be a certain way or be perfect to come to God and truth be told if we know how to fix our life, we wouldn't need Jesus. I thought so too but I was so messed up and did not know it until God shines his spotlight on me and I started to see all my dirt. We always think we are ok/right but the only one who can show us otherwise is the one who created us, and we know he has a manual for every one of us. Trust him to be the potter in our lives and put us back together.

Again, come no matter how broken you are he can mend the broken pieces and put us back together again piece by piece and will give us just what we need as we go along. Trust the God that has the blueprint for our life, he is waiting for you.

All I can say is that God is true to his word, and we have to lead by example, watch what we do even when no one is looking because it's easy to be good when everyone is looking but can you maintain that same standard when you are alone? You see, I came to Christ with a made-up mind and was sick and tired of being sick and tired, so it was easy once I fell in love with Jesus. I didn't say the journey was easy, I said, "Because I fell in love with Jesus." I would meet him every night at a set time, and no one could interrupt my time with the Lord, and everyone knows after a certain time, don't come and don`t call. It's me and Jesus' time to the point that my neighbor's downstairs were being healed. I didn't know that my prayers were helping someone until the person gave my son a letter and then another letter came about how my prayers echo in their apartment and help them. I wear Jesus everywhere I go; I am not ashamed of him nor am I ashamed to talk about him every opportunity I get.

I had two other neighbors separated from the one downstairs and one of them would use something to knock on my roof from their apartment telling me to move my bed. One day I said to the Lord, "What is this Jesus?" First of all, I was living there first, and I was not about to interrupt my meeting place with Jesus. I asked Jesus to fix it. My intentions were not to disturb my neighbors, but they were so rude. I attended an AIM Convention in Orlando, Florida for a couple of days and when I got back, they were gone. God took care of that. The next tenants moved in but this time they were the ones disturbing my prayers. Again, I just said, "Really Jesus." and the next thing I know they were moving too. The third person God sent there needed everything I was praying for, and I did not know until I got the letters I mentioned earlier. Not only did she send me letters she invited me to lunch, sent little gifts upstairs to me, and when we met for lunch that's when she opened up to me and told me what she was going through and how my prayers from upstairs had been helping her. A new door was opened for me to minister to her, and I did.

God sees everything, the first two tenants did not want the prayers and the Lord sent someone who needed and appreciate the prayers. Everything that God does, if we just allow him to because he won't force himself on us. He gives us free will and does everything well. He knows what is needed in any given situation and again we just have to trust him by activating our faith and relinquishing control. Give God control of our life every step of the way. God is a great God with a sense of humor. I really think he didn't have to allow the second tenant who was going to disturb me, but he knows me so well and what I was going to say, "I think Jesus will do things just for the fun of it." He knew I was going to look up to heaven and say, "REALLY JESUS." Lol.

From time to time my kids would hear me talking and ask me, "Mom who are you talking to?" and then they would say, "Oh I forget Jesus (smile). Yes, they know me, I remember one day the kids beg me to watch a movie and they know I don't watch just any movie. It has to be clean and represent Jesus, so one of my sons bought a movie and told me he looked at it first and it's clean and you will like it. What I did not know when they set it up for me to watch, they went into their rooms, they were watching my response to the movie from one corner of the room. I did enjoy the movie it was clean just like my son said and it made them happy to see me laughing.

First, I was single at that time and saved and did not intend to give the enemy anything, so my children know what I do inside my house is the same thing I do outside so it's easy when you live an open life, you never have to pretend. I always tell people what you see with me, that is what you get. There is no pretense or anything phony about me. Jesus came in and he redeemed and cleanse me from the inside out.

In Hindsight:

This transition in my life was and is not easy. I could feel myself dying but still alive meaning everything that we think we are and have learned to be will change. When God gets a hold of us nothing can stay the same. It's like God has to give us a spiritual bath and the bath lasts as long as the stuff that is on us takes to come off. Even though God has saved us we still have to go through the pruning process, and no one likes it, but you cannot get that beautiful oil called olive oil unless the olives were squeezed and even crushed. It hurts sometimes.

I wondered when this will all end but God kept adding strength where it was necessary. Believe me, when God is in the fire with us, we will be like Shadrach, Meshach and Abednego in Daniel: 3:26. "Keep the faith), God is not through with me yet and one thing is for sure, two things for certain, we will come out as pure gold if we allow God to finish what he started in us. Many times, I felt like giving up, walking away, but when I look back on the pain I have already endured in my life, I can see the difference now, at least I know God is with me and he's the one training me.

Basically, I had to make up my mind that I won't quit. I love God too much and now that I have tasted his goodness, how could I turn back, and turn back to what, and for what? I just must continue to die to myself daily until there is no more of me left and take it from me, I am nowhere near or even close. Every day I see something else in me that needs to die. I must put my flesh on the cross every day and believe me some days it is not on the cross some days I choose to keep it and then I realize how dangerous it can be to not die to my flesh daily. I want to be used by God so in order to be used by God I have to get out of God's way.

Allow God back on his throne and let God be God. He knows what we need, he knows what we can bear, so even when we think the road is too hard for us God always knows when to show up.

Take God at his word because I learned I can do it the easy way or the hard way. One way or another God's will eventually will be done in our lives.

In Hindsight:

The end will never come until all of God's children come to play nice at home. God's Way, God's time and God's perspective.

Learn to color between the lines for the perfect work of art.

Acknowledgment

All My Children - Sarnia, Locksley, Audley & my two
deceased sons Marlon & Huffeno, Marlon my firstborn,
Huffeno my fourth-born son.

Apostle Warren Martin, Apostle Barbera Martin, Bishop
Patrick Benjamin, Evangelist Shields, Pastor Zelma,
Evangelist LaDonna, Amber Ettienne

And to all those who touch my life along the journey,
whether in a positive or negative way, Thank You all.

About the Author

Pastor Benaiah Harris

Born in Kingston, Jamaica on the 5th of October 1963.
Mother of 5, Grandmother of 7 and 1 great grandchild.
Benaiah Ministers and leads a Prayer Line as she was led
by her Father in Heaven. Her free time is spent feeding the
homeless, time with family, traveling and quiet time with
God.

Seeds of Blessings Ministry-Prayer Line

Thank you for reading my book and I pray you are blessed. This ministry allows all believers to be led by the Spirit of God in all we do according to Romans 8:14 "For as many as are led by the Spirit of God, they are the Sons of God" (KJV).

Seeds of Blessings is owned and directed by the servants of God, truly living in the word. The ministry was gifted to me but is owned by the Lord Jesus Christ. We worship God in spirit & truth while loving one another the way he intends it. We uphold each other and pray for the needs of the people near to us as well as afar. In the end, we are in the mission of winning SOULS for the Kingdom of God.

Seeds of Blessings always represent, 2 Corinthians 9:10, "Now he that ministered seed to the Sower both minister bread for your food and multiply your seed sown and increase the fruits of your righteousness" (KJV).

This ministry has allowed me to speak at Christian Engagements and will one day be gifted in a building while continuing the prayer line. As Christians, having all the support out hear with things like the prayer line, allows us to keep our faith and continue this fight for GOD. Soul saving is what I am blessed to do and happily serve in any way I am called to do.

Join us here: Mondays, Wednesdays, & Fridays at 9:00 p.m. ET. Please dial: 681-999-0192 Access Code:372263

Made in the USA
Middletown, DE
19 March 2022

62665488R00045